NORTHERN LIGHTS

Renae Gilles and
Warren Rylands

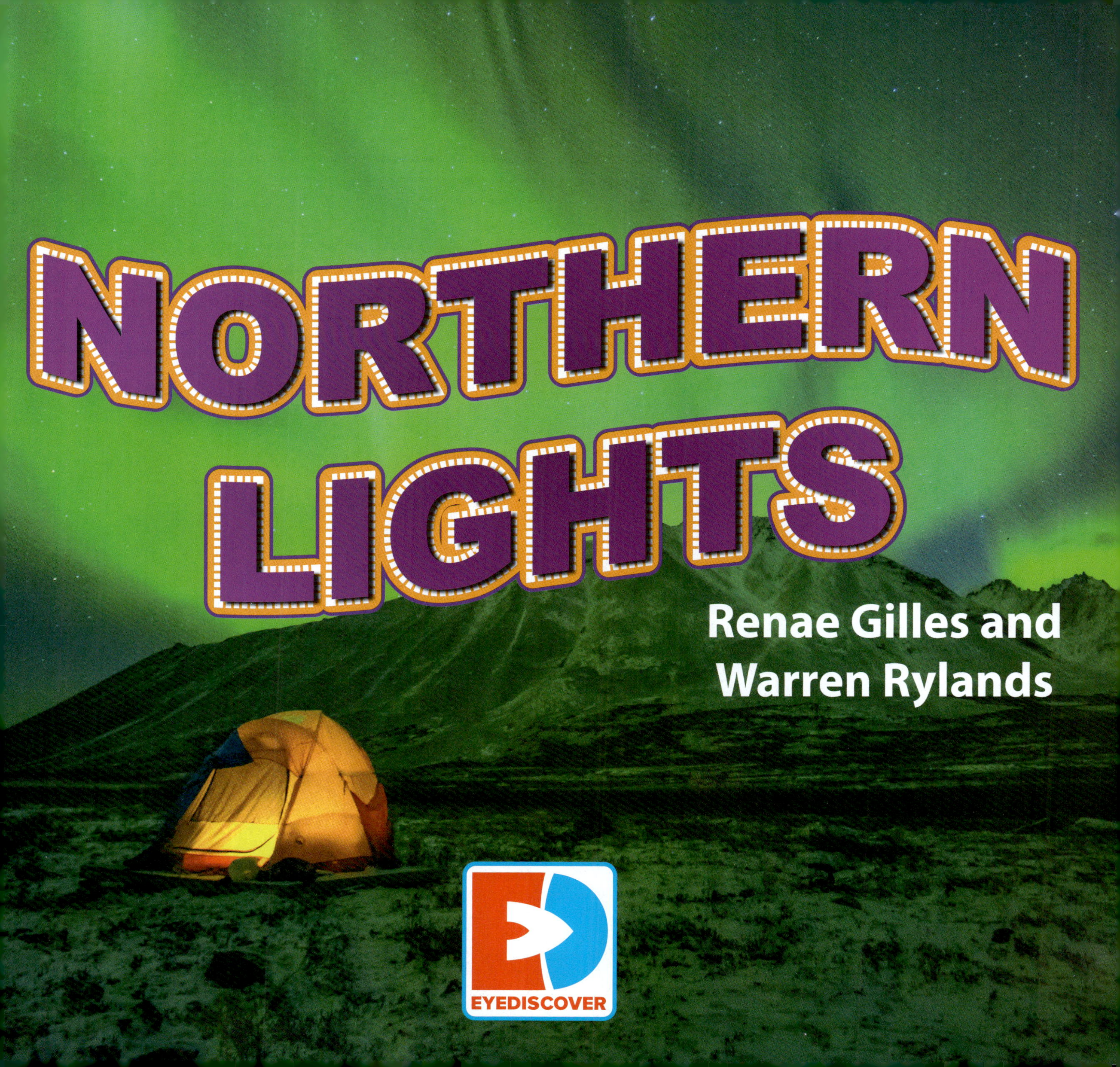

EYEDISCOVER

EYEDISCOVER

Go to **www.eyediscover.com** and enter this book's unique code.

BOOK CODE

AVY35575

EYEDISCOVER brings you optic readalongs that support active learning.

Published by AV² by Weigl
350 5th Avenue, 59th Floor New York, NY 10118
Website: www.eyediscover.com

Library of Congress Control Number: 2018951112

ISBN 978-1-4896-8011-2 (hardcover)

Printed in the United States of America
in Brainerd, Minnesota
1 2 3 4 5 6 7 8 9 0 22 21 20 19 18

082018
120917

Project Coordinator: John Willis
Designer: Mandy Christiansen

Weigl acknowledges Getty Images, iStock, Shutterstock, and Wikimedia as the primary image suppliers for this title.

EYEDISCOVER provides enriched content, optimized for tablet use, that supplements and complements this book. EYEDISCOVER books strive to create inspired learning and engage young minds in a total learning experience.

Watch
Video content brings each page to life.

Browse
Thumbnails make navigation simple.

Read
Follow along with text on the screen.

Listen
Hear each page read aloud.

Your EYEDISCOVER Optic Readalongs come alive with...

Audio
Listen to the entire book read aloud.

Video
High resolution videos turn each spread into an optic readalong.

OPTIMIZED FOR

- ✓ TABLETS
- ✓ WHITEBOARDS
- ✓ COMPUTERS
- ✓ AND MUCH MORE!

NORTHERN LIGHTS

In this book, you will learn about

- how they look
- where they are
- what they do

and much more!

The northern lights are streaks of color in the night sky.

There are many stories about the lights. One says they are animal spirits.

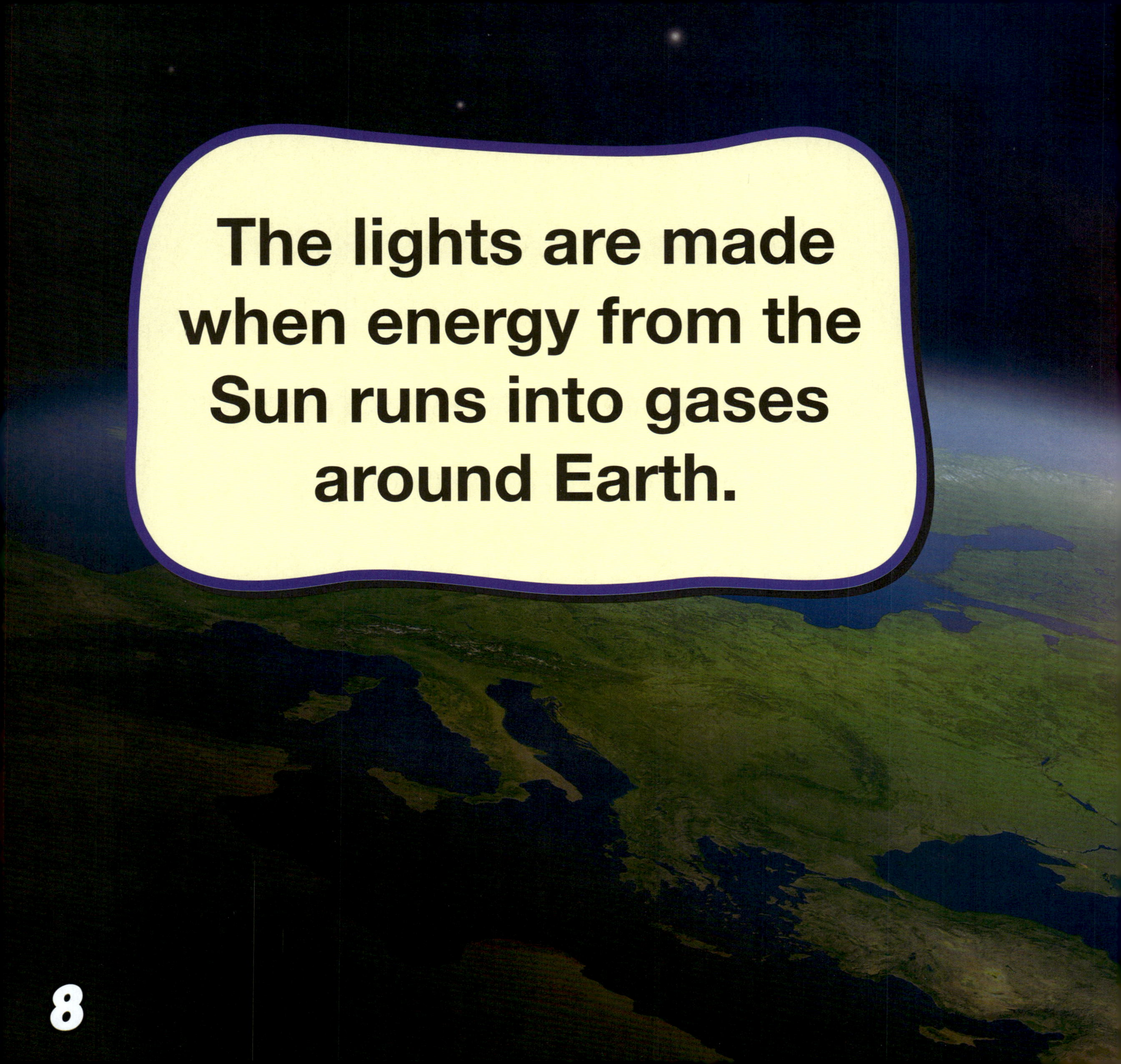

The lights are made when energy from the Sun runs into gases around Earth.

Different gases make different colors. The lights can be green, red, yellow, pink, or blue.

Many people travel to places such as Alaska to see the lights.

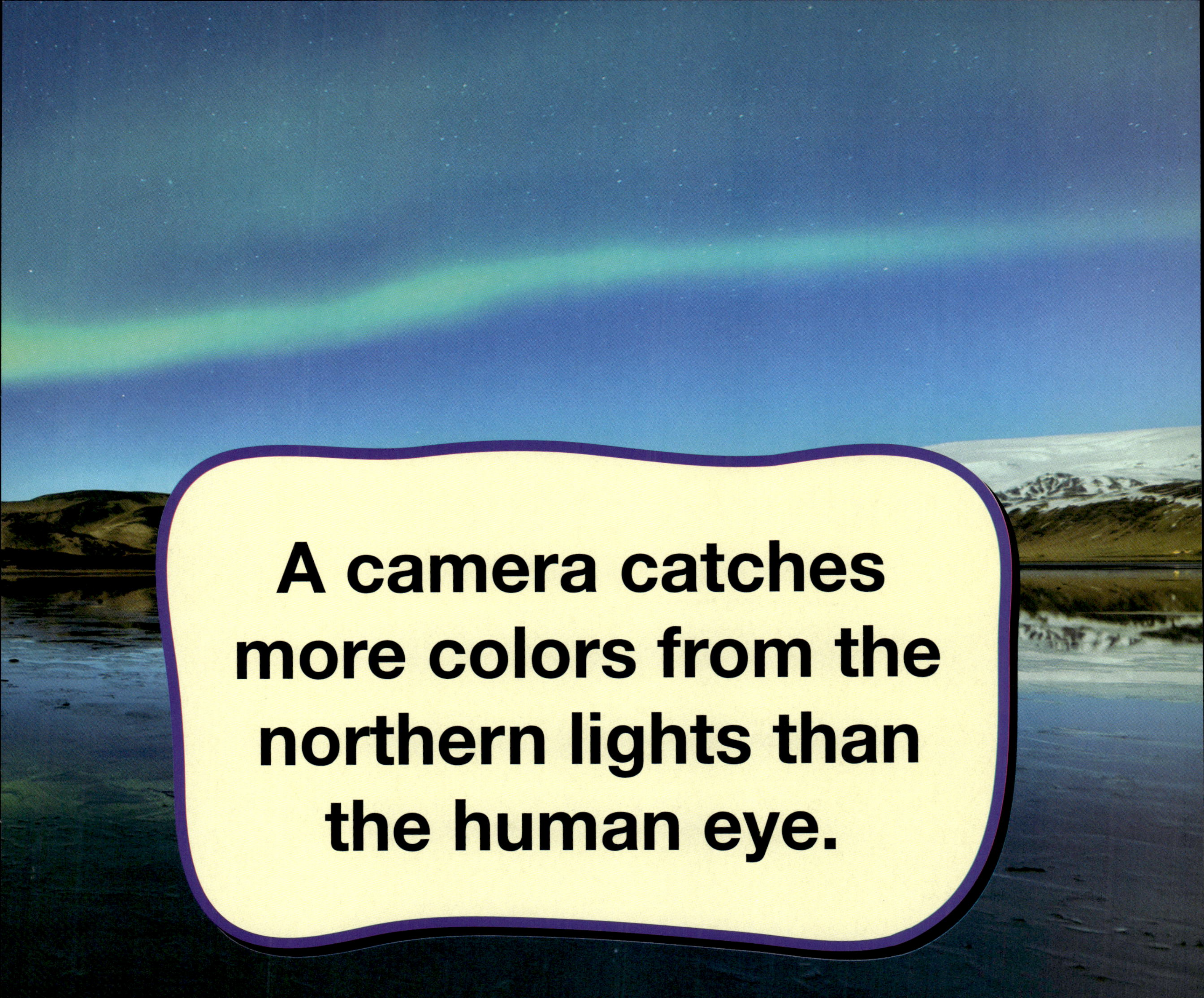

A camera catches more colors from the northern lights than the human eye.

The northern lights can be seen from space. Astronauts take pictures of them.

There are northern lights on other planets, too. Jupiter, Saturn, Uranus, and Neptune have them.

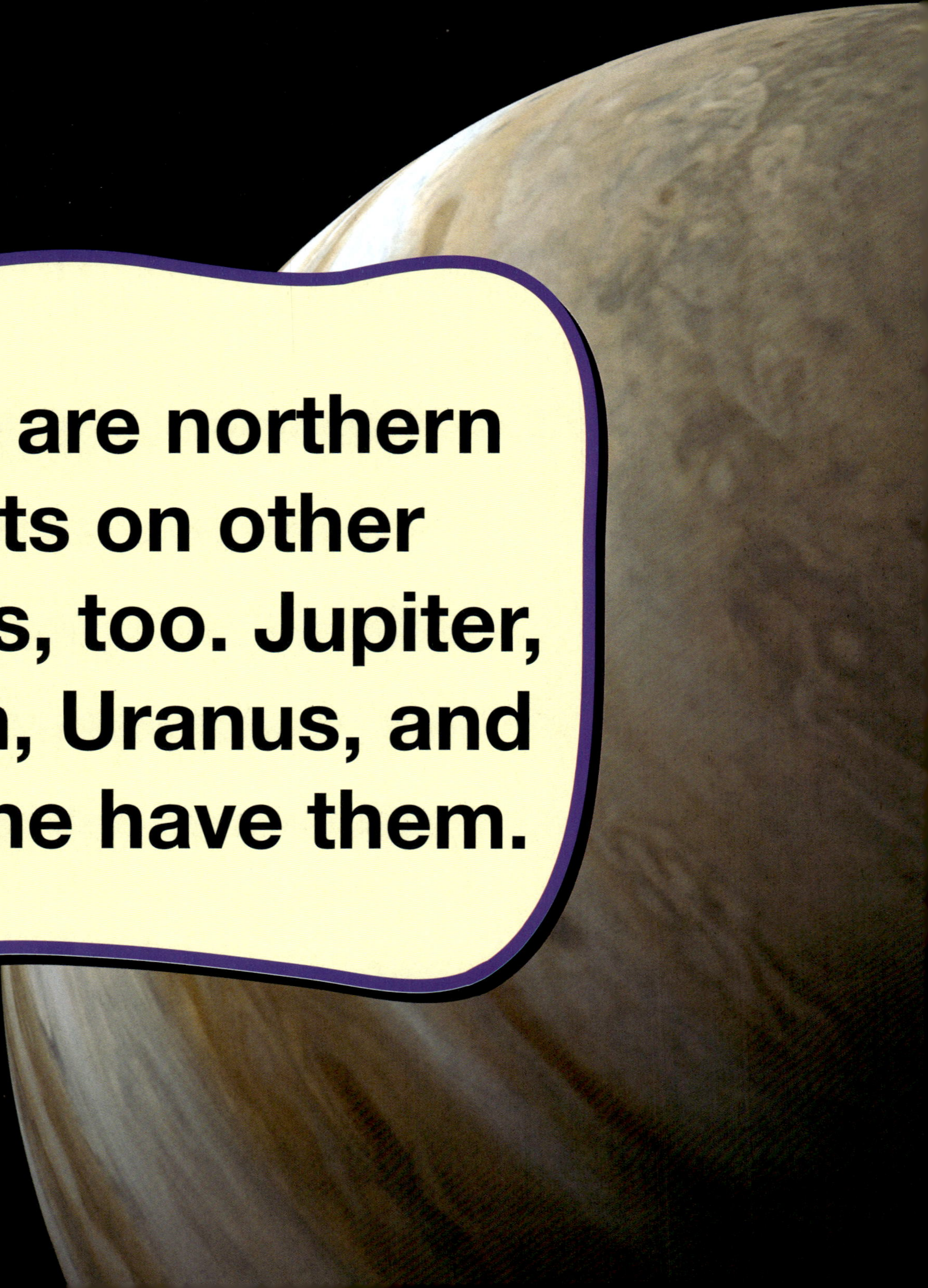

The northern lights are beautiful. People have watched them for thousands of years.

NORTHERN LIGHTS BY THE NUMBERS

Cave paintings from 30,000 years ago show the northern lights.

The northern lights can best be seen in Alaska between 10 p.m. and 2 a.m.

The lights are 60 to 600 miles above the ground.

(97 to 970 kilometers)

No **two** northern lights are the **same**.

It takes energy from the Sun **two** or **three days** to reach Earth.

Earth is

93 million

miles from the Sun.

(150 million km)

KEY WORDS

Research has shown that as much as 65 percent of all written material published in English is made up of 300 words. These 300 words cannot be taught using pictures or learned by sounding them out. They must be recognized by sight. This book contains 38 common sight words to help young readers improve their reading fluency and comprehension. This book also teaches young readers several important content words, such as proper nouns. These words are paired with pictures to aid in learning and improve understanding.

Page	Sight Words First Appearance
4	are, in, night, of, the
7	about, many, one, there, they
8	around, Earth, from, into, made, when
11	be, can, different, make, or
12	as, people, see, such, to
15	a, more, than
16	take, them
18	and, have, on, other, too
20	for, years

Page	Content Words First Appearance
4	color, northern lights, sky, streaks
7	animal, spirits, stories
8	energy, gases, Sun
11	blue, green, pink, red, yellow
12	Alaska
15	camera, eye, human
16	Astronauts, pictures, space
18	Jupiter, Neptune, planets, Saturn, Uranus

Watch
Video content brings each page to life.

Browse
Thumbnails make navigation simple.

Read
Follow along with text on the screen.

Listen
Hear each page read aloud.

EYEDISCOVER

Go to www.eyediscover.com and enter this book's unique code.

BOOK CODE

AVY35575